P9-DNU-167

LET'S-READ-AND-FIND-OUT SCIENCE®

STAGE 1

Animals in WINTER

by Henrietta Bancroft and Richard G. Van Gelder
illustrated by Helen K. Davie

HarperCollins*Publishers*

The *Let's-Read-and-Find-Out Science* book series was originated by Dr. Franklyn M. Branley, Astronomer Emeritus and former Chairman of the American Museum–Hayden Planetarium, and was formerly co-edited by him and Dr. Roma Gans, Professor Emeritus of Childhood Education, Teachers College, Columbia University. Text and illustrations for each of the books in the series are checked for accuracy by an expert in the relevant field. For more information about Let's-Read-and-Find-Out Science books, write to HarperCollins Children's Books, 10 East 53rd Street, New York, NY 10022.

HarperCollins®, ☂®, and Let's Read-and-Find-Out Science® are trademarks of HarperCollins Publishers Inc.

ANIMALS IN WINTER
Text copyright © 1997 by The Estate of Henrietta Bancroft
and The Estate of Richard G. Van Gelder
Illustrations copyright © 1997 by Helen K. Davie
All rights reserved. No part of this book may be used or reproduced in any manner whatsoever without written permission except in the case of brief quotations embodied in critical articles and reviews. Printed in the United States of America.
For information address HarperCollins Children's Books, a division of HarperCollins Publishers,
10 East 53rd Street, New York, NY 10022.

Library of Congress Cataloging-in-Publication Data
Bancroft, Henrietta.
    Animals in winter / by Henrietta Bancroft and Richard G. Van Gelder ; illustrated by Helen K. Davie.
        p.   cm. — (Let's-read-and-find-out science. Stage 1)
    Summary: Describes the many different ways animals cope with winter, including migration, hibernation, and food storage.
    ISBN 0-06-027157-4. — ISBN 0-06-027158-2 (lib. bdg.). — ISBN 0-06-445165-8 (pbk.)
    1. Animals—Wintering—Juvenile literature. [1. Animals—Wintering.   2. Winter.]   I. Van Gelder, Richard George, date   II. Davie, Helen, ill.   III. Title.   IV. Series.
QL753.B26   1997   95-36246
591.54'3—dc20   CIP
                                                                                                                                    AC

Typography by Elynn Cohen
2   3   4   5   6   7   8   9   10
❖
Revised Edition

Animals in WINTER

The days grow short. The nights grow long.
It is getting colder. Winter is coming.

4

Leaves have fallen from the trees. There are no berries on the bushes. Insects are gone. The grass is dead and brown.

Birds and other animals are getting ready for winter. Some of the birds will fly south. Bluebirds and orioles go toward the south.

They go where it is warm and sunny and where there is food for them to eat. When spring comes, the birds will make the long journey back north. They migrate.

Some butterflies migrate, too. That is what the monarch butterflies do.

They gather in a tree by the hundreds before cold weather comes. They stay in the tree all night. In the morning, they fly toward their winter homes in the south.

Many bats fly south, too. But some bats stay in the north all winter. When the weather gets cold, they go to a cave. There is no wind or snow in the cave. The bats sleep there all winter.

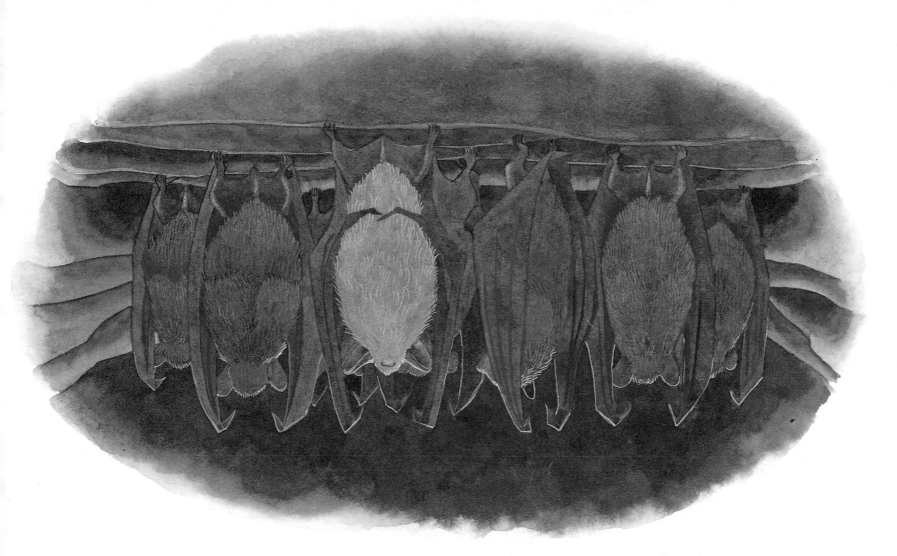

They do not eat. They live on fat stored inside them.
They do not move. They hardly breathe. They sleep,
sleep, sleep.
They hibernate.

Woodchucks hibernate, too. When fall comes, a woodchuck eats and eats and eats. He eats grass, twigs, and leaves. He grows fat. When it gets cold, the woodchuck crawls into his long tunnel and goes to sleep.

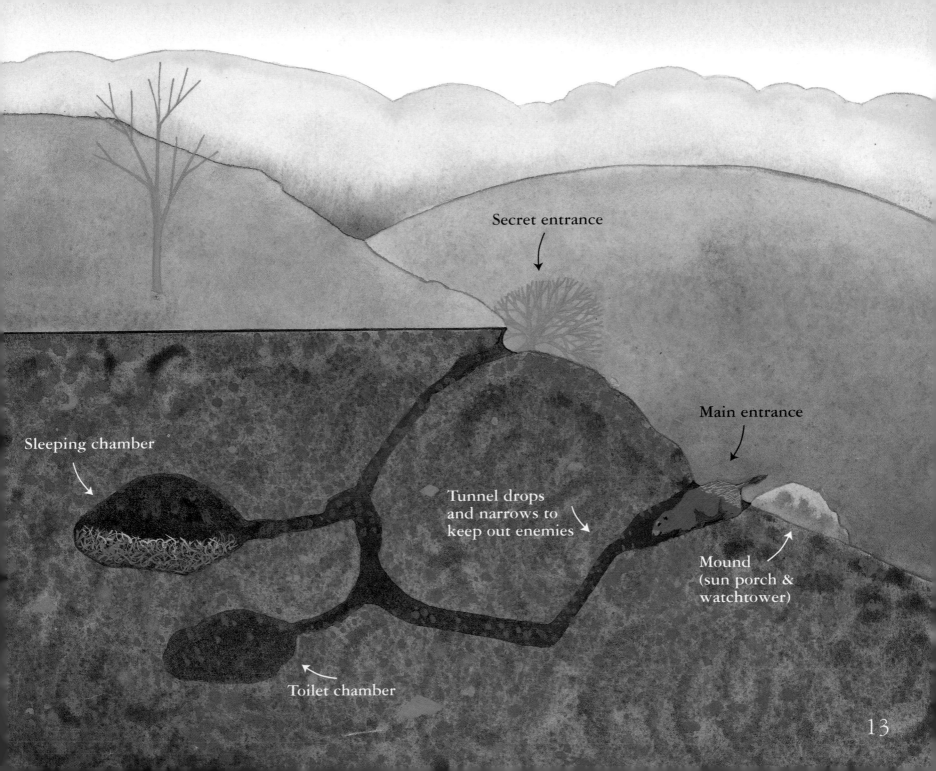

Secret entrance

Main entrance

Sleeping chamber

Tunnel drops
and narrows to
keep out enemies

Mound
(sun porch &
watchtower)

Toilet chamber

13

| December | January | February | March |

Does he sleep for a day? Longer than that.
Does he sleep for a week? Longer than that.
A month? Even longer! A woodchuck can
sleep as long as four months!

14

The woodchuck seems hardly alive. He breathes very slowly. His heart beats slowly. He sleeps, sleeps, sleeps. He hibernates.

Some animals do not have to hibernate. They gather
food and save it for the winter.

That is what a pika does. A pika looks a little like a rabbit, but with round ears. Pikas live in high mountains where winters are long and cold. They eat grass. In summer they cut more grass than they can eat. They spread the grass on flat stones. The hot sun dries it.

By the end of summer, a pika
may have gathered fifty pounds
of grass. She hides it under rocks.
In winter she eats the dry
grass. It keeps her alive.

18

Squirrels gather food, too, and save it for winter.
They dig holes in the ground. They bury hickory
nuts and acorns.

When winter comes, they dig them up and eat
them. Sometimes squirrels forget where they buried the nuts.
Trees may grow from the nuts that squirrels forget.

Some animals do not get ready for winter at all. They do not store food. They do not hibernate. They do not migrate. They must hunt for food all winter long.

22

There are mice that must hunt all winter for seeds of goldenrod, asters, and other wild plants. Sometimes they eat farmers' corn, oats, and wheat.

23

Deer must dig in the snow for dried leaves, plants, and moss. When the snow is deep, they must eat the twigs, buds, and bark of trees.

The rabbit must hunt under the snow for bits of
grass and plants. When the snow is deep, he, too,
eats the buds and bark of bushes so he can stay alive.

In the winter, the fox hunts for mice and rabbits.

This fox has discovered a mouse in its tunnel beneath the snow.

When the winter is cold and the snow is deep, many animals cannot find food. Here are some ways you can help animals in winter.

Stick fruit and cheese pieces on a dead branch.

Hang suet in a plastic net bag.

Make a peanut-and-popcorn garland.

Nail a seed tray with drainage holes to a fence post.

Nail a sunflower head to a post or fence.

Make an apple, cranberry, raisin, and orange garland.

Make sure feeders are placed out of reach of predators.

Put a birdhouse in a tree or under the eaves of your house.

Hang an ear of corn for squirrels and chipmunks.

Plant shrubs with berries for food and shelter.

Please remember: Once you begin feeding birds and other wild animals in winter, you must continue. They are depending on the food you supply.

31

Eventually, the days grow longer. The nights grow shorter. It begins to get warmer. Spring is coming.

32

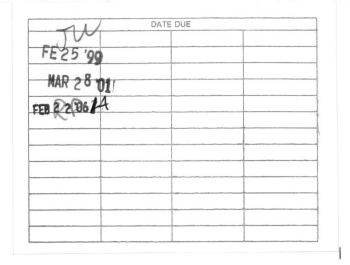

DATE DUE			
FE 25 '99			
MAR 28 01			
FEB 22 06			

591.56
BAN

Bancroft, Henrietta.

Animals in winter

YAVNEH DAY SCHOOL LIBRARY

753411 01489   45259A